RIDE THE RAILS

Contents

Written by Ben Lerwill

Collins

1 Riding the rails

Let's begin with a funny-looking steam engine. It had yellow wheels and a chimney as tall as a giraffe. Its name was Rocket – and it helped to change the world.

The train was part of the first-ever railway to connect two cities. It travelled between Manchester and Liverpool, in England, in 1829.

Today, trains are found in almost every country. In sunshine or snow, they rumble along the rails, carrying people and **goods** where they need to go.

Just like Rocket all those years ago, they connect places.

The very earliest railways had small **wagons**, pulled by humans or animals. From the 1830s, most **locomotives** were steam engines, using burning coal.

By the 1950s, electricity and **diesel** had taken over. Since then, our trains have become faster, longer and more powerful.

Today, we have trains that cross jungles, islands and mountains. We have trains that rattle through tunnels under the sea. We have city trains, desert trains and trains that can pull hundreds of wagons at the same time.

All trains run on railway tracks.

These tracks are usually made from **steel**, with wooden, steel or **concrete sleepers** underneath.

Railway tracks can be difficult to lay. Sometimes, tunnels have to be blasted into rocks, and bridges have to be built across valleys.

Other tracks curve beneath cliffs or climb big hills.

FACT

Worldwide, there are more than 1.3 million **kilometres** of railway tracks. That's nearly enough to stretch to the moon and back – twice!

2 Tremendous trains

The world's longest train journey is on the Trans-Siberian Railway in Russia. It takes up to seven days – passengers have their own beds!

The Qinghai-Tibet Railway goes so high into the mountains that **oxygen** is piped into carriages, to help passengers breathe!

Eurostar trains travel between England and France in a 50-kilometre tunnel under the sea!

The Shanghai Maglev has a record speed of 501 kilometres per hour – more than four times quicker than a sprinting cheetah!

One of the most amazing things about trains is how different they can be.

This train in Thailand trundles right through a busy market.

This train in Italy rolls onto a special ferry to reach the island of Sicily.

This train in Bolivia has been made from an old bus.

Some trains are like palaces on wheels. The Blue Train is a famous South African train with polished carriages, bow-tied waiters and big, soft beds.

Which train looks the most fun to you?

Not all trains carry passengers. Freight trains move heavy goods and containers from one place to another.

They can carry everything from cars, corn and chemicals to coal, cows and cans of food.

FACT

Some freight trains cover more than 1,000 kilometres in a day.

The longest train ever was an Australian freight train pulling 682 wagons – it was as heavy as 20,000 elephants!

Australia has lots of very long freight trains.

3 Drivers and Stations

Drivers have an important job. They control how fast trains go and where they stop. They have to check the track **signalling** and make sure their trains pull safely into stations.

Look at all the different dials and buttons!

Most railways also have guards, or conductors. They check tickets, help passengers and keep the trains running on time.

Guards wear different uniforms in different countries. Some guards have special caps, colourful flags and very loud whistles.

FACT

The world's busiest station is Shinjuku Station in Tokyo, Japan. More than 2.7 million people use it every day!

The station with the longest name is in North Wales. It's called (deep breath) Llanfairpwllgwyngyllgogery-chwyrndrobwllllantysiliogogogoch.

India has some very grand stations.
Just look at Charbagh Railway Station!

The world's oldest underground station is Baker Street, in London. It opened in 1863. Today, around 200 cities worldwide have their own underground railways. Two of the most famous are the Paris Métro, which has more than 300 stations, and the New York Subway, which has more than 470!

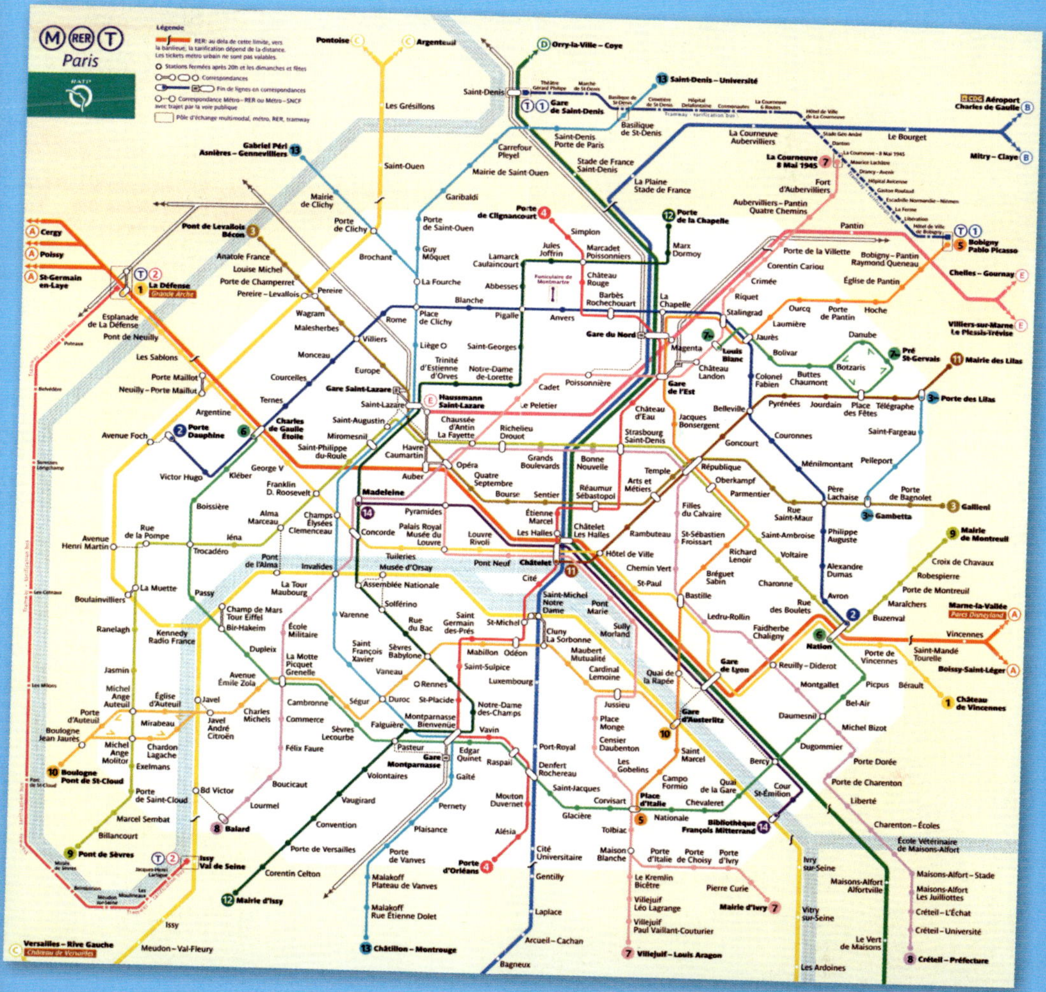

Trains and railways have starred in some very famous books and films. How many of them do you know?

In the Harry Potter books, the Hogwarts Express departs King's Cross Station, in London, from Platform 9¾.

Marmalade-loving Paddington Bear gets his name after being found on a platform at London's Paddington Station.

The Polar Express is a train that speeds through the night on Christmas Eve to reach the North Pole.

The first Thomas the Tank Engine books rolled into bookshops in 1945.

Trains still help people all around the world to travel quickly and comfortably. They're better for the **environment** than aeroplanes and most cars.

Trains have been with us for hundreds of years, but they have a BIG role to play in the future.

Glossary

concrete a substance used for building which is made by mixing together cement, sand, small stones, and water

diesel a fuel that some trains use to power their journeys

environment the air we breathe and the planet we live on

goods everything carried by train that isn't a passenger, for example, coal or logs

kilometres units of length; one kilometre equals 1,000 metres

locomotives the engines pulling the rest of the train

oxygen a gas in the air, without which we can't breathe properly

signalling a system of lights to control trains, similar to traffic lights

sleepers the supports under a train track

steel a strong metal, partly made from iron

wagons special vehicles attached to a train for carrying goods

Index

A world of rail

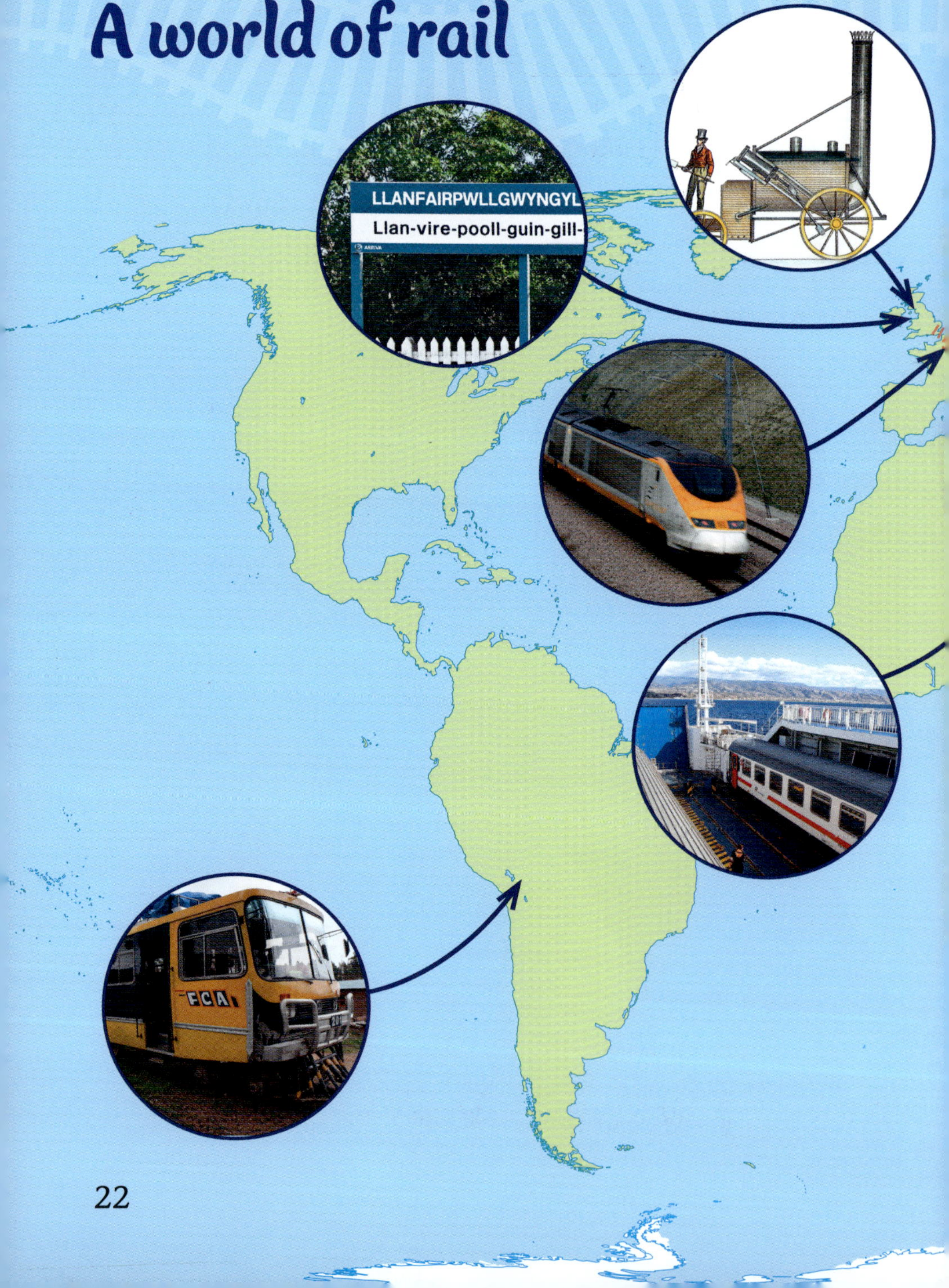

Ideas for reading

Written by Gill Matthews
Primary Literacy Consultant

Reading objectives:

- discuss and clarify the meanings of words, linking new meanings to known vocabulary
- answer and ask questions
- participate in discussion about books, poems and other works that are read to them and those that they can read for themselves, taking turns and listening to what others say

Spoken language objectives:

- articulate and justify answers, arguments and opinions
- give well-structured descriptions, explanations and narratives for different purposes, including for expressing feelings
- maintain attention and participate actively in collaborative conversations, staying on topic and initiating and responding to comments

Curriculum links: Science – geographical skills and fieldwork

Word count: 894

Interest words: goods, guards, sleepers, tracks

Resources: internet access, large sheets of paper

Build a context for reading

- Show children the front cover of the book. Ask them to find and read the title and the author's name.
- Ask them to describe what they can see on the front cover.
- Read the back-cover blurb aloud. Explore children's experiences of train travel. If necessary, describe a train journey that you have made.
- Point out that this is an information book. Ask children what they know about information books and what they think they will find in this one.
- Open the book at the contents page. Ask children what a contents page is for and how it is organised. Challenge children to find Chapter 3 *Drivers and stations* by opening the book to where they think p14 might be.